THE

C000000683

DUBLIN MONUMENTS
AND SCULPTURE TRAIL

ELIZABETH HEALY

WOLFHOUND PRESS
& in the US and Canada
The Irish American Book Company

First published in 1998 by
Wolfhound Press Ltd
68 Mountjoy Square
Dublin 1, Ireland
Tel: (353-1) 874 0354
Fax: (353-1) 872 0207
Published in the US and Canada by

The Irish American Book Company
6309 Monarch Park Place
Niwot, Colorado 80503
USA
Tel: (303) 652-2710
Fax: (303) 652-2689

Wolfhound Press receives financial assistance from the Arts Council/An Comhairle
Ealaíon, Dublin.

British Library Cataloguing in Publication Data
A catalogue record for this book is available from the British Library.

ISBN 0-86327-637-7

10 9 8 7 6 5 4 3 2 1

Editorial Consultant: Roberta Reeners
Design and Origination: Design Image
Cover Illustration: Nicola Emoe
Cover Design: Slick Fish Design, Dublin
Printed in the Republic of Ireland by Colour Books, Dublin

For permission to reproduce photographs, the publishers are grateful to Bord
Fáilte/The Irish Tourist Board and Rod Tuach.

CONTENTS

The Monuments
of Dublin

Dublin is a fortunate city in many ways. Its setting, at the foot of the Dublin/Wicklow mountains, gives it a special vibrancy. The bay sends salt air into the heart of the city, and the heather-clad hills appear to rise from the ends of the city streets.

Dublin grew from a Viking settlement below Christchurch Cathedral in the ninth century, and the streets of that area still echo the street plan of the earliest expansion. Through the Middle Ages, the city clustered around Dublin Castle and the two cathedrals – one inside the city walls, the other outside, both founded by the Anglo-Normans who held Dublin, if precariously, from the beginning of the twelfth century. Settlement gradually spread across the Liffey: the earliest bridge was built around the year 1000.

After the Elizabethan conquest, Dublin felt secure enough to expand north and eastwards. The eighteenth century saw the great Georgian development of Dublin, when its wide streets, fine squares and most elegant buildings were created.

A city's monuments reflect its history. The heroes and heroines it chooses to honour and the events it commemorates may change with the ebb and flow of circumstance, and monuments may tumble as regimes change. But by and large, the

DUBLIN MONUMENTS

story can be read from those monuments which preside over the changing scene and those which are added as time goes by.

In recent decades, more corporate and decorative sculpture has come to ornament the streets. The trend was given particular impetus during Dublin's Millennium Year, 1988, and during 1991 when Dublin was European City of Culture.

The struggle for independence has been Ireland's chief political preoccupation and Dublin's major monuments reflect that fact. Some of these are ranged along the centre of O'Connell Street, but this tour begins a short distance north of it, at Parnell Square.

The area covered in this Guide is roughly speaking the city centre, with a foray out to St Patrick's Cathedral in the oldest part of Dublin, and another in the opposite direction to the Grand Canal. The limits are to some degree arbitrary, taking in what would be considered reasonable walking distance though doing it in a few 'bites'. A few important outlying monuments are included as well.

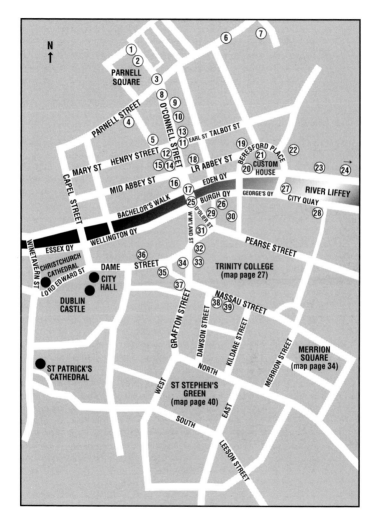

Parnell Square and
O'Connell Street

1. THE GARDEN OF REMEMBRANCE

Near the top corner of Parnell Square is a quiet water-garden withdrawn from the traffic. A stretch of water leads to a large sculpture backed by a curved wall which carries an inscription in Irish, with an English translation on a separate plaque.

The garden is dedicated 'to those who gave their lives in the cause of Irish freedom'. The later stages of that centuries-old struggle, after the 1916 Easter Rising and the subsequent War of Independence, ended with a Treaty which created the

Irish Free State (Ireland has since achieved the status of Republic) but allowed the six north-eastern counties, commonly referred to as Ulster, to remain part of the United Kingdom. The consequences of that arrangement have, unfortunately, not yet been fully resolved.

The sculpture (opposite) depicts 'The Children of Lir', an image from an ancient Irish legend in which four children were turned into swans by their wicked stepmother. They remained so for 900 years, but kept their sweet singing voices. Oisín Kelly's bronze echoes the idea expressed by W.B. Yeats when he wrote of this struggle for freedom: 'All changed, changed utterly: A terrible beauty is born.'

Garden designed by Daithí P. Hanley. Bronze sculpture by Oisín Kelly. Lettering by Michael Biggs and Philip O'Neill. Opened in 1966.

2.   THE IRISH VOLUNTEERS

Close by on the grassy margin is a small plinth showing a symbolic broken chain, and fronting a struggling ash tree. It commemorates the Irish Volunteers, founded at a meeting here in the Rotunda Gardens in 1913. The Irish Volunteers were formed in response to the Ulster Volunteers, a group established to resist the creation of an Irish Free State. The Irish Volunteers formed the nucleus of the force which staged the Rising of 1916. (See also No. 1 above.) By Werner Schrermann. Erected 1960.

3. PARNELL

Parnell's fine monument stands on the central island where Parnell Street crosses the top of O'Connell Street. The inscription reads:

> *No man has a right to fix the boundary to the march of a nation. No man has a right to say to his country 'Thus far shalt thou go and no further.' We have never attempted to fix the ne plus ultra to the progress of Ireland's nationhood and we never shall. Go soirbhighidh Dia Éire dá clainn.*
> *[That God may make Ireland flourish for her people.]*

Charles Stewart Parnell (1846-91), one of Ireland's greatest constitutional leaders, was often referred to as 'The Uncrowned King of Ireland'. Though a well-to-do Protestant landowner, he placed himself at the head of a movement which achieved extensive agrarian reform, very much against the interests of his own class. The failure of his campaign to secure Home Rule for Ireland, along with a scandal arising from his association with a married woman, Katharine O'Shea, brought tragedy at the end of his life. He died in 1891 at the age of forty-five. Over 200,000 people followed his funeral to Glasnevin Cemetery.

The monument was executed in New York by Dublin-born sculptor Augustus Saint-Gaudens. Unveiled 1911. On the same day, Dublin Corporation changed the name of Great Britain Street to Parnell Street.

Before moving on down O'Connell Street, two diversions are recommended for modern sculpture enthusiasts, one westward, the other to the east.

At the junction of Parnell Street and Moore Street stands THE GREEN LIGHT (4), a slender lamp inspired by the street traders of Moore Street. Fish hang from its crossbar; vegetables and fruit are arrayed around it; discarded banana peels lie scattered about. By Rachel Joynt, 1992.

At the other (south) end of Moore Street, a colourful mosaic among the street cobbles (5) celebrates the Moore Street Market with fruit and flower motifs. By Orla Kelly and Bernard Rocca, 1993.

In Summerhill, in the opposite direction (following Parnell Street eastwards), is a nice fluid piece suggesting dancing children (6). Bronze on stone by Cathy Carmen, 1991.

In a small cul-de-sac at Portland Row (turn right further along Summerhill), two small bronze figures mingle with the flesh-and-blood children who play there (7). By Fred Conlon, 1991.

---

8. SACRED HEART SHRINE

Dublin taxi-drivers have been located in this part of O'Connell Street for many years and the small red shrine  housing a statue of the Sacred Heart is known generally as 'the Taxi-Drivers' Shrine'. It was erected by the taxi-drivers around the time of the Eucharistic Congress in 1932, when religious fervour was high and many shrines were made in homes and in public places. This one is still tended and cared for by Dublin taxi-drivers.

---

9. FATHER MATHEW

Father Theobald Mathew (1790-1856), 'the Father of Temperance', stands in his Capuchin robe. Leader of the early nineteenth-century campaign for total abstinence, his temperance movement led to dramatic social changes. (It might appear to visitors to Dublin that some of his influence has worn off in the century since!) By Mary Redmond, 1889.

---

10. ANNA LIVIA FOUNTAIN

The River Liffey, in Irish *Abha an Life*, transmuted into 'Anna Livia', was further expanded by James Joyce into 'Anna Livia Plurabelle'. Always personified as a woman, here she lies in

repose, the water flowing along her contours. The fountain wasn't long in place before Dubliners' often unkind wit had her named 'the Floozie in the Jacuzzi', 'the Bride in the Tide' and 'the Whore in the Sewer' (in Dublinese, the words rhyme). But they're slowly becoming fond of her.

Fountain designed by Sean Mulcahy. Anna Livia sculpture by Eamon O'Doherty, 1988.

11. NELSON'S PILLAR

It could be said that the most notable statue in O'Connell Street is the one that isn't there. In the small hours of Tuesday, 8 March 1966, Nelson and his pillar were blown up 'by persons still officially unknown'.

For a century and a half, Nelson's Pillar had been an icon of Dublin city. The magnificent Doric column, 36 metres (120 feet) high, was surmounted by a statue of Admiral Horatio Nelson. It dominated the principal thoroughfare of the capital and was a distinctive feature of all depictions of the city.

'The Pillar' had always been a controversial monument. In the early 1800s, the proposal to erect a monument to the Hero of Trafalgar seemed insensitive to say the least, especially at a period when Ireland was undergoing such radical political and social change. Following independence,

there were regular resolutions to substitute a national figure for that of Nelson. Ultimately, the controversy was otherwise resolved.

Various odds and ends of the consequent debris were collected and preserved. Some of the great base blocks with fine lettering have ended up in the courtyard of the Kilkenny Design Workshops in that city. The immense head now resides in the Dublin Civic Museum at 58 South William Street, close to Grafton Street in the city centre.

12. CÚCHULAINN

The bronze statue of Cúchulainn stands inside the central window of the General Post Office, commemorating the men of the 1916 Easter Rising. The GPO was their headquarters, and an Irish Republic was declared from its steps. In the event, it took another thirty-two years to achieve the formal status of Republic.

Cúchulainn is a mythical Irish hero-figure. When mortally wounded, he tied himself to a pillar-stone so that he could die facing his enemies. So feared was he that his enemies would not approach until they saw a raven, the symbol of death, alight on his shoulder. By Oliver Sheppard, 1934.

13. JAMES JOYCE

Here he is in characteristic pose near the corner of North Earl Street, leaning jauntily on his stick. James Joyce (1882-1941) is perhaps Ireland's most famous writer, though the number of books written *about* him vastly outweighs his own output.

The statue by Marjorie Fitzgibbon was unveiled by the Lord Mayor on 'Bloomsday' 1990. Bloomsday is 16 June, the day on which, in 1904, the events recounted in *Ulysses* take place. Every year, the action of the novel is followed around the streets of Dublin by hordes of literary pilgrims as the city indulges in various lively and entertaining diversions.

See also The Joyce Walk, page 30.

14. JAMES LARKIN

The inscription quotes his rallying-cry:

The great appear great because we are on our knees: let us rise.

James 'Big Jim' Larkin (1876-1947) was the founder of Ireland's Trade Union movement. A big, vigorous man with a colourful personality, he is shown on a tall plinth in a typical pose, addressing a public meeting in O'Connell Street. In the early years of the twentieth century, the poverty of Dublin's tenement slums was notorious. Larkin's demand for Trade Union recognition, directed at the city's most powerful employers, led to the dramatic strike and lock-out of 1913. Larkin was succeeded by James Connolly, founder of the Irish Citizen Army, which joined the Irish Volunteers in the 1916 Rising. (See Nos. 2 and 20.) By Oisín Kelly. Unveiled 1979.

15. SIR JOHN GRAY

Gray (1816-75) was a member of Dublin Corporation and was knighted for, among other public services, promoting Dublin's Vartry water supply scheme. A liberal Protestant nationalist, he used his newspaper, the *Freeman's Journal*, to promote such causes as religious freedom and free denominational education. He also supported Daniel O'Connell's Repeal movement. (See O'Connell, No. 17.) By Sir Thomas Farrell. Unveiled 1879.

16. WILLIAM SMITH O'BRIEN

O'Brien (1803-64) was one of the leaders of a group of romantic and idealistic young nationalists called Young Ireland. After the failure of Daniel O'Connell's constitutional Repeal movement (No. 17), they instigated an abortive rebellion in 1848. Smith O'Brien was sentenced to death, commuted to transportation to Australia.

The statue by Sir Thomas Farrell stood originally (1870) at the junction of Westmoreland Street and D'Olier Street. Regarded as a traffic hazard, it was moved to this position in 1929.

17. DANIEL O'CONNELL

The great 'Liberator', Daniel O'Connell (1775-1847) is one of the giants of Irish history, and the size of the monument, with its guardian angels (Winged Victories representing Patriotism, Fidelity, Courage and Eloquence), reflects the

fact. A brilliant constitutional lawyer and orator, a man of
monumental energy, he secured the amelioration of the
restrictive code under which the Catholic population of
Ireland suffered at the time, including the right to enter

parliament. This, of course, was the British parliament, because an Irish one didn't exist after 1800, when a short-lived independent Irish parliament was abolished by the Act of Union of Ireland with Great Britain.

Because he taught the poor and the landless that there was power in numbers, he was sometimes called 'the King of the Beggars'.

Following Catholic Emancipation, O'Connell's second great popular campaign was for the Repeal of the Act of Union and the restoration of an Irish parliament. He was a committed pacifist and his Repeal movement collapsed when he called off a 'monster' meeting after it was proscribed, as he feared its consequences. This failure and the tragedy of the Famine, it is said, broke his heart and led to his death four years later.

The erection of the monument was itself a saga. Almost thirty years elapsed between the time such a monument was proposed and its completion in 1882, eighteen years after the foundation stone was laid. In the meantime, eighty designs had been rejected and its final designer, John Henry Foley, had died before it was finished, leaving the final stages to his principal assistant, Thomas Brock.

As an additional historical footnote, notice the bullet-hole in the bosom of the winged figure of 'Courage'. It is a souvenir of the War of Independence.

EAST & SOUTH OF O'CONNELL STREET

Back-track a short distance on O'Connell Street and turn right (eastwards, that is down-river) into Lower Abbey Street. A little distance along, on the left, is TALKING HEADS (18). The little group of three heads on pillars is a playful comment on the nearby Abbey Theatre and the waiting bus-queue. By Carolyn Mulholland, 1989.

Continuing along Lower Abbey Street, the Irish Life Centre is on the left. Ahead is the Custom House, the great classic building on the river.

19. IRISH LIFE CENTRE

There are several works associated with the Irish Life complex. Of those in the public area, the most dramatic is THE CHARIOT OF LIFE, a magnificent sculpture of a charioteer and galloping horses (opposite). It is intended to symbolise the struggle of reason to control the forces of passion. By Oisín Kelly, 1982.

SWEENEY ASTRAY, a Venetian glass mosaic mural, is in a quiet garden area reached by a flight of steps on the left of the building. It illustrates the story of King Sweeney, made mad by the curse of a saint. A version of the ancient story has been translated by Ireland's Nobel Laureate, the poet Seamus Heaney. By Desmond Kinney, 1987.

20. JAMES CONNOLLY

The Trade Union leader stands outside the railings of the Custom House. The memorial shows the Plough and the Stars flag of the Irish Citizen Army, participants in the 1916 Rising. Connolly (1868-1916) was executed for his part in the Rising. The memorial faces the 'new' Liberty Hall, Trade Union headquarters. Monument by Eamon O'Doherty, 1996.

21. MOTHER IRELAND

Beside the pond on the Custom House lawn, a personified figure of Ireland holds a dying soldier. By Yann Renard Goulet. Lettering by Michael Biggs. 1955.

22. AMNESTY

On the traffic island in the centre of the triangle formed by
the Custom House, Busaras (the bus station) and the AIB
International Financial Centre, Amnesty has raised a fitting
monument, 'Universal Links for Human Rights'. A globe of
iron chains encloses an eternal flame. The legend reads: 'The
candle burns not for us but for all those whom we failed to
rescue from prison, who were tortured, who were kidnapped,
who disappeared. That is what the candle is for.' By Tony
O'Malley, 1995.

23. FAMINE GROUP

Continue down to the river front and turn eastwards (down-
river) along Custom House Quay. A little distance along the
quay, by the waterside, a pathetic procession of ragged, half-

starved figures clutching little bundles of possessions struggles along, followed by a skin-and-bone dog. It is a reminder of Ireland's famine, one of a number of memorials created for the 150th anniversary of those terrible years. From here, the hungry and dispossessed took ship for hoped-for better lives elsewhere. By Rowan Gillespie, 1997.

24. THE MARINER

A good 10-minute walk along the North Wall Quay leads to Maritime House on the corner of Castleforbes Road where a jolly bronze sailor holds an anchor. It was erected to mark the official opening of Maritime House, headquarters of a number of shipping agencies. By John Behan, 1973.

25. THE PEOPLE'S ISLAND

At the southern end of O'Connell Bridge, where D'Olier Street and Westmoreland Street converge, note the footprints on the ground, an amusing assemblage of shoes, bare feet, birds and other imprints. By Rachel Joynt, 1988.

26. THE SHEAHAN MEMORIAL

On the corner of Hawkins Street and Burgh Quay, a monument surmounted by a cross commemorates a strange and tragic accident which occurred in 1905. One John Fleming opened a manhole and descended into a 7-metre (23-feet) deep sewer to investigate a broken pipe. He was overcome by deadly fumes. In the ensuing attempts at rescue, twelve workers were hospitalised and one, Patrick Sheahan, died himself, having rescued several others.

27. MATT TALBOT

Farther down-river, on City Quay by the corner of Matt Talbot Memorial Bridge, a granite statue honours the Venerable Matt Talbot (1856-1925) for whom the bridge is also named. A man of noted sanctity and patron of the city docks, he worked for many years in the Dublin Port and Docks Board. By James Power, 1988.

28. THE SEAMEN'S MEMORIAL

Two blocks further along the quay, in front of a small park, a large bronze sea-anchor backed by a granite pillar honours the memory of the seamen lost while serving on Irish Merchant ships during the years 1939 to 1945. Their names are listed, together with the names of the ships which were lost. Erected 1990.

29. THE STEYNE, OR LONG STONE

At the top (southern end) of D'Olier Street, on a grass island (sometimes flower bed) on College Street, stands the 'new' Steyne. The Norse Vikings, who established a settlement that

grew to be the city of Dublin, set their symbolic pillar-stone or Steyne on the spot where they first landed (the Liffey was much wider then). It was 3 metres (10 feet) high and stood there for some 800 years – until about 1720.

The spot was subsequently occupied by a memorial to Surgeon Sir Philip Crampton (1777-1858). That 6-metre (20-feet) floral sculpture, justly likened to a rotting pineapple, was not grieved over when it was damaged by traffic and removed in 1959. The 'new' Steyne by Cliodna Cussen was erected in 1986. Its story is told on a small plinth which is, alas, almost totally illegible.

---

30. Close by, outside the Screen Cinema, is the amusing figure of MR SCREEN, sculpted by Vincent Browne, 1988.

---

31. THOMAS MOORE

Moore (1779-1852) stands in his wind-swept cloak on the traffic island facing the Bank of Ireland at College Green, his back to a now-disused public convenience. 'Moore's Melodies' are still sung in many parts of the world: 'The Last Rose of Summer', 'The Harp that Once...', 'The Minstrel Boy' and many others. He was Ireland's best-loved poet and his songs were potent icons of Irish

patriotism. In Joyce's *Ulysses*, Mr Bloom irreverently remarks to himself that they did right to put him up over a urinal: meeting of the waters. By Christopher Moore. Erected 1857.

32. EDMUND BURKE

Edmund Burke (1729-97), statesman, orator and writer, stands with his hand on his hip outside the front gate of Trinity College. A graduate of Trinity, Burke figures among the great names in the history of political literature and philosophy. He was a passionate advocate of civil and religious liberties in Ireland, Britain and the colonies, including America. Among his best-known works is *Reflections on the Revolution in France*. By John Henry Foley. Erected 1868.

❋ *Burke*

❋ *Goldsmith*

33. OLIVER GOLDSMITH

On the other side of the gate, another Trinity graduate, Oliver Goldsmith (1728-74), stands with an open book. So well he might, it has been remarked, since he rarely opened one during his days in Trinity. Goldsmith, 'who wrote like an angel and spoke like poor Pol', idled away his youth and failed to graduate. His long-suffering

family sent him to Edinburgh to try for a degree in medicine, where he started to write to supplement his income and, probably, to pay his debts. Thereafter he produced some of the great masterpieces of the English language: *The Vicar of Wakefield, She Stoops to Conquer, The Deserted Village* etc. There is a memorial to him in the Poets' Corner in Westminster Abbey. By John Henry Foley. Erected 1864.

34. HENRY GRATTAN

* *Grattan*

Grattan (1746-1820), statesman and orator, stands opposite Burke and Goldsmith in the centre of a traffic island, his arm upraised as if, somebody remarked, he was inviting the pair to a very lively party. Among Grattan's most notable achievements was the securing of a semi-independent parliament for Ireland in the eighteenth century which, unfortunately, lasted for only a short period. He is buried in Westminster Abbey. By John Henry Foley. Erected 1876.

COLLEGE GREEN

35. **THOMAS DAVIS**

When this memorial was unveiled in 1966, there was considerable controversy. Nearly everybody approved of the fountain (usually dry nowadays) which depicts the Heralds of the Four Irish Provinces. But the powerful figure of Davis met with grave reservations in a city more used to traditional representations of its heroes – especially as young Thomas Davis (1814-45) carried quite a romantic image. The statue's monumental style reflects the power of Davis's intellectual and political vigour. He was a poet and one of the founders of the *Nation*, a journal which became the voice of the movement known as Young Ireland, of which he was a leader. (See William Smith O'Brien, No. 16.) The editorial excellence of the *Nation* also helped to encourage the beginnings of an Irish literary revival. Tragically, Davis died when only thirty years of age, but his influence far outlasted his short, active life. Sculptor, Edward Delaney. Lettering, Michael Biggs. Erected 1966.

36. **CRANN AN ÓR (The Golden Tree)**

The 7-metre (23-feet) high bronze tree with its granite awning, in front of the Central Bank, is intended to symbolise the nation's wealth and the bank's part in husbanding it! By Eamon O'Doherty, 1991.

GRAFTON STREET

37. MOLLY MALONE

> *As she wheels her wheelbarrow*
> *Thro' streets broad and narrow*
> *Crying 'Cockles and Mussels,*
> *Alive alive-o.'*

There she is, the much-sung fishmonger of Dublin's Fair City, offering her wares ... in more ways than one. A few coins are often to be seen caught in her cleavage. Dubliners know her as 'the Tart with the Cart'. By Jeanne Rynhart, 1988.

NASSAU STREET

In the Setanta Centre, next to the Kilkenny Shop, there are two items.

STEEL CONSTRUCTION (38) by Gerda Fromel (1974) is a tall, convoluted form reflecting the light.

The ceramic mural on the theme of THE TÁIN (39) is by Desmond Kinney, also 1974. *The Táin* is an ancient epic prose tale of cattle-raiding, treachery and hero-exploits. The principal warrior is Setanta (later renamed Cúchulainn), after whom the Centre is named. (See also No. 12, Cúchulainn, GPO.)

A wall-plaque quotes the querulous footnote of the monk-scribe of the twelfth-century manuscript, in which he dismisses the whole story as something 'for the enjoyment of idiots'.

TRINITY COLLEGE

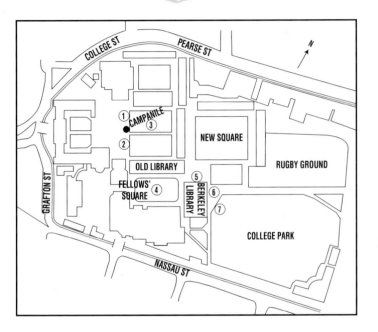

There are some important sculptures in the grounds of Trinity College. Entering by the main gate on College Green, the two memorial statues flanking the campanile ahead are of George Salmon and William Lecky.

1. GEORGE SALMON

The Rev. Dr George Salmon (1819-1904), mathematician and theologian, graduate of Trinity, was Provost from 1888

until his death in the Provost's House in 1904. By John Hughes, 1911.

---

2. WILLIAM LECKY

Lecky (1838-1903), historian and philosopher, was also a Trinity graduate and author of the *History of Rationalism* and *The Map of Life*. His widow endowed the Lecky Chair of History to the college and left all his papers to its archives. By Sir Wm Goscombe John, 1911.

---

3. RECLINING CONNECTED FORMS

Henry Moore's marvellous convoluted bronze form stands (or lies?) in an inconspicuous position on the lawn behind the campanile. 1969.

4. **CACTUS**

The huge black steel construction by the renowned sculptor Alexander Calder stands in Fellows' Square. It was donated by a graduate. 1967.

5. Arnaldo Pomodoro's magnificent SFERE CON SFERE (Sphere with Sphere, 1982) stands in the podium of the Berkeley (new) Library. It was donated by the artist, with the support of Trinity College and Italian organisations in Ireland.

6. An untitled MARBLE SCULPTURE by Geoffrey Thornton, donated by the artist, stands amid the shrubbery at the side of the Berkeley Library in College Park.

7. COUNTERMOVEMENT, a wood sculpture by Michael Warren (1985), donated by the American Irish Foundation, is also in College Park.

THE JOYCE WALK

For literary pilgrims, fourteen pavement plaques trace the route of Leopold Bloom, the central character in James Joyce's *Ulysses*, from the newspaper office in Middle Abbey Street where he worked (now the offices of *The Irish Independent*), down O'Connell Street, across the river, along Westmoreland Street on the left-hand side, past Thomas Moore's statue, up Grafton Street, into Duke Street where he lunched in Davy Byrne's pub, across Dawson Street and on to the National Museum in Kildare Street.

The plaques, each bearing the relevant quotation from the eighth chapter of *Ulysses*, were created by Robin Buick, 1988.

MERRION SQUARE

Leinster House (seat of the Government), the Natural History Museum and the National Gallery of Art make up the west side of Merrion Square.

1. Occupying the central position on the lawn of Leinster House is a pillar surmounted by a flame, a monument to THE FOUNDERS OF THE IRISH STATE – Michael Collins, Kevin O'Higgins and Arthur Griffith. By Raymond McGrath, F. du Berry and Laurence Campbell.

2. To the left is a memorial to PRINCE ALBERT by John Henry Foley. It was once accompanied by a large statue of Queen Victoria with retinue which stood on the site where the central memorial is now, until it was taken down in 1948. It eventually made its way to Australia.

3. A fountain close by is to the memory of Surgeon EDWARD STAMER O'GRADY.

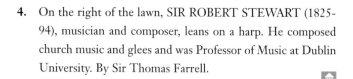

4. On the right of the lawn, SIR ROBERT STEWART (1825-94), musician and composer, leans on a harp. He composed church music and glees and was Professor of Music at Dublin University. By Sir Thomas Farrell.

5. The memorial in front of the National Gallery is to WILLIAM DARGAN (1799-1867), railway entrepreneur and 'arch-improver' of his time, by whose efforts the Gallery was built. The statue is by Thomas Farrell.

   A statue of George Bernard Shaw (by Troubetsky) which stood outside for many years has been taken in out of the cold and now stands indoors in the Shaw Room. The Gallery has reason to be grateful to Shaw, since he left it one-third of the royalties from his published works. He said that the Gallery provided him with the best part of his education.

6. MAJOR THOMAS HEAZLE PARKE (1857-93), surgeon, of Drumsna, Co. Leitrim, is the man commemorated in front of the Natural History Museum. As a member of the Royal Army Medical Corps, he carried out some remarkable expeditions in Egypt and Africa. The plaque on the pedestal shows him saving the life of an expedition's engineer by sucking out the venom from a poisoned arrow, in traditional adventure-story fashion.

7. Directly facing the National Gallery is what is still known as the RUTLAND FOUNTAIN, though no water flows in it. Dating from 1791, it was restored in recent times and commemorates the Duke of Rutland (1754-87), Viceroy to Dublin, 'the only Chief Governor', according to the architect James Gandon, 'who could find leisure to pay the least attention to the Fine Arts'.

Merrion Square – more properly Archbishop Ryan Park – was a private park for the use of residents of the surrounding houses until 1930 when it was acquired by the Roman Catholic Archbishop of Dublin who intended to build a cathedral there. It was never built, however, and in 1974, Archbishop Ryan made the park over to Dublin Corporation 'as a garden and recreation for public use'. It is a pleasant and restful place, quieter than St Stephen's Green except perhaps during weekday lunch-hours.

The Square boasts an interesting collection of old street lamps, making it almost a museum of these relics of former times. Notice also the use of old tree roots as natural sculptures.

The handful of memorials and decorative sculptures in Merrion Square mostly appear to lurk amongst the shrubbery, providing opportunities for an interesting game of hide-and-seek. The map on page 34 provides a self-guided tour.

8. Enter by one of the small gates facing Leinster House and turn left. In the corner, poet and dramatist OSCAR WILDE (1854-1900) reclines languidly on a large quartzite boulder.

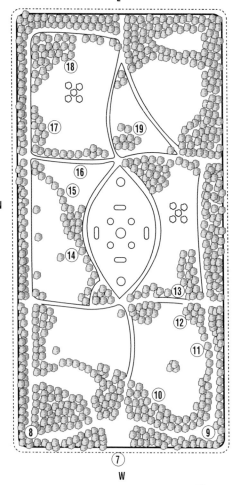

He faces across towards No. 1 Merrion Square where he lived as a youth with his remarkable and eccentric parents – Sir William, eye and ear specialist, archaeologist, antiquarian and philanderer; and Lady Wilde, who wrote passionately nationalistic verse under the pen-name 'Speranza'. Appropriate to his character, the author of *The Importance of Being Earnest* and *Lady Windermere's Fan* is made from exotic and beautifully coloured stone including jade, granite and porcelain. Nearby are two bronzes on plinths representing art and life and bearing quotations from other Irish writers. By Danny Osborne, 1997.

9.   Walking anti-clockwise, in the south-west corner is the sombre and hauntingly tragic group called THE VICTIMS. Two sorrowing figures stand over one lying injured or dead: the inevitable innocent victims of war. Bronze by Andrew O'Connor. Installed 1976. The sculptor lived for some time at No. 77 Merrion Square.

10. GEORGE RUSSELL (Æ)

Known as Æ, George Russell (1867-1935) was poet, artist, mystic, agriculturist – a strange mixture in a large man with a large personality. His paintings show spirits of the earth and air, while his practical side managed the Agricultural Organisation Society. The AOS's offices were once at No. 84 Merrion Square. By Peter Grant, 1985.

11. In the shrubbery nearby, a cherry tree planted by the Irish Campaign for Nuclear Disarmament on Hiroshima Day, 6 August 1980, commemorates the victims of that terrible event.

12. MICHAEL COLLINS

Revolutionary and statesman, hero of the War of Independence, Collins (1890-1922) was tragically shot in the Civil War which followed. A man of great physical courage and force of personality, Collins was one of the team which negotiated the Anglo-Irish Treaty of 1921. He was chairman of the Provisional Government and, during the Civil War, commander-in-chief of the government forces. Many believe that, had he lived, the subsequent history of Ireland may have been less troubled. By Dick Joynt, 1988.

13. HENRY GRATTAN

Orator and parliamentarian, Grattan (1746-1820) was the leader of the short-lived semi-independent Irish parliament which governed Ireland prior to the Act of Union in 1800. By Peter Grant, 1982.

14. BERNARDO O'HIGGINS

General and statesman, O'Higgins (1778-1842) is known as the 'Liberator of Chile'. His father had risen from humble Irish origins to become Major-General in the Chilean army.

After his death, Bernardo led the successful movement for independence from Spain. The memorial was presented by the Republic of Chile to Ireland in 1995.

15. THE TRIBUTE HEAD

The bronze head by Elizabeth Frink was unveiled in 1983 to commemorate the twentieth year of Nelson Mandela's imprisonment and as a mark of support for the struggle against apartheid in South Africa. The monument was donated by Artists for Amnesty.

16. In the centre of the lawn, a Japanese maple planted in 1997 honours WILLIE BERMINGHAM, the Dublin fireman who, twenty years previously, founded Alone, an organisation which cares for elderly people living alone.

17. ÉIRE

A fine work by Jerome Connor, installed here in 1976. In myth and in poetry, Ireland has been traditionally personified as a noble female. Notice the fine lettering in the inscription at the back of the stone.

18. THE TREE OF LIFE

Eavan Boland's poem is inscribed in stone in the north-east corner of the Square. It is dedicated to the babies who died at birth in the National Maternity Hospital just across the road in Holles Street. Intended as a place of quiet and meditation, a service is held there occasionally for the mothers of these children.

19. MOTHER AND CHILD

A semi-abstract granite sculpture by Patrick Roe, 1985.

ST STEPHEN'S GREEN

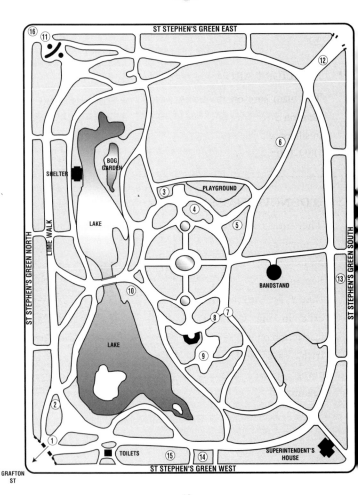

St Stephen's Green was open commonage until 1663, after which it was enclosed and gradually surrounded by buildings. It was laid out as a public park in 1880 through the liberality of Sir Arthur Guinness, Lord Ardilaun. (See No. 14, below.)

1. FUSILIER'S ARCH

The main gate on the north-western corner, by the top of Grafton Street, is a memorial to the men of the Royal Dublin Fusiliers who fell in the Boer War in South Africa during 1899-1902. Erected 1907.

2. O'DONOVAN ROSSA

The massive uncut boulder of Wicklow granite commemorates Jeremiah O'Donovan Rossa (1831-1915),

prominent member of the Fenians, who edited the *United Irishman* while in exile in the USA. The inscription on the plaque, in Irish, says 'Ireland will never forget you.' By Seamus Murphy. Erected 1954.

The next seven items are arrayed around the central lawns and fountains of the Green.

3. THOMAS KETTLE

Poet and patriot, Kettle (1880-1916) was killed in the Battle of the Somme in 1916. The lines inscribed are from a sonnet which he wrote for his daughter:

> *Died not for flag, nor King, nor Emperor,*
> *But for a dream, born in a herdsman's hut,*
> *And for the sacred scripture of the poor.*

By Albert Power, 1937.

4. THE HASLAMS

A stone bench commemorates Anna Maria (1829-1922) and Thomas Haslam (1825-1917) and their work for the enfranchisement of women. Erected 1925.

5. COUNTESS MARKIEVICZ

Constance Gore-Booth (1868-1927) was one of the aristocratic Gore-Booth family of Lissadell, Co. Sligo, which features in the work of the poet W.B. Yeats. A major in the Irish Citizen Army, Constance was sentenced to death for her part in the 1916 Rising. Her sentence was later commuted to penal servitude for life, although she was released in 1917. She was the first woman to be elected a member of the British parliament. By Seamus Murphy, 1956.

6. FIANNA ÉIREANN

A stone plinth, somewhat hidden by shrubbery behind the children's playground, commemorates the youth movement founded by Countess Markievicz, many of whose members participated in the Rising of 1916. Erected 1966.

7. MANGAN

James Clarence Mangan (1803-49) was regarded by many as the finest poet before Yeats. A tragic figure, alcoholic and opium-addicted, he lived in dire poverty and died of malnutrition and cholera. A small marble head set into a niche in the pedestal represents *Róisín Dubh* or 'Dark Rosaleen', a symbolic name for Ireland and the title of one of Mangan's best-known works. The Mangan bust is by Oliver

Sheppard; the 'Dark Rosaleen' piece is the last work of Willie Pearce, one of those executed after the 1916 Rising. Erected 1909.

---

8. MAGDALEN BENCH

To the memory of women whose lives, as single mothers, were spent in the Magdalen Laundry Institutions during the first half of this century, under very harsh conditions. Irish society has come to feel remorse for the treatment of these women. Erected 1995.

---

9. YEATS

Close by, some steps lead to a secluded paved platform area where stands a fine sculpture by Henry Moore entitled KNIFE EDGE. With its flowing lines and graceful sense of movement, it fittingly commemorates the poet William Butler Yeats (1865-1939), one of Ireland's Nobel Laureates. Erected 1967.

---

10. BENNETT and CHENEVIX

A bench which forms part of the garden for the blind commemorates two women who worked together for women's rights, social justice and world peace, Louie Bennett and Helen Chenevix. By Francis Barry, 1958.

Other major monuments are located around the periphery of St Stephen's Green.

11. WOLFE TONE (1763-98) stands at the gateway of the north-east corner. Tone is regarded as the founder of Irish republicanism (below, left). He was a leading member of the Society of United Irishmen which instigated the Insurrection of 1798. Tone was convicted of treason and sentenced to death by hanging, but died in prison apparently of a self-inflicted wound.

Behind the lofty stone wall screen (which has earned the monument the designation 'Tonehenge') is THE FAMINE GROUP (page 45), commemorating that tragic period of 1845-48. By Edward Delaney. Erected 1967.

12. THE THREE FATES

A little inside the south-east corner, a fountain reflects this fine sculpture by Josef Wackerle which was presented by the people of the Federal Republic of Germany to the people of Ireland in gratitude for their help after World War II. The three female bronze figures represent the legendary Fates, spinning and measuring the thread of human destiny. Erected 1956.

13. JAMES JOYCE

Half-way along the south side, a bust of James Joyce (1882-1941) reminds us that Stephen Dedalus, hero of *Portrait of the Artist as a Young Man*, tells of 'Crossing Stephen's, that is, my green'. By Marjorie Fitzgibbon, 1982.

Just outside, on the roadside, a BENCH is a further tribute to Joyce and to his father, John Stanislaus Joyce. It faces Newman House, where Stephen Dedalus spent much time discussing weighty topics in the same novel. The bench was placed here in 1977. (See also pages 11 and 30.)

Two memorials on the west side of the Green are best viewed from the road outside.

14. LORD ARDILAUN

In a small railed-off section, Sir Arthur Guinness (1840-1915) of the brewing dynasty, later Lord Ardilaun, is commemorated as the philanthropist who had the old common of St Stephen's Green laid out as gardens and beautified 'for the use and enjoyment of the citizens of Dublin'. By Thomas Farrell, 1892.

15. ROBERT EMMET

'Bold Robert Emmet, the darling of Erin' goes the song. Another romantic patriot, Emmet (1778-1803) was executed for leading a rebellion, this one in 1803. He was just 25 years old. The statue by Jerome Connor is a replica of one in Washington DC. Here, it faces the site of the house where Emmet was born. By Jerome Connor, 1968.

16. Outside the north-east corner of the Green, on the traffic island opposite the Wolfe Tone monument (across the road from the Shelbourne Hotel), is TRACE, paired archways

echoing the shape of Georgian doorways. By Grace Weir, 1988.

SOUTH OF
ST STEPHEN'S GREEN

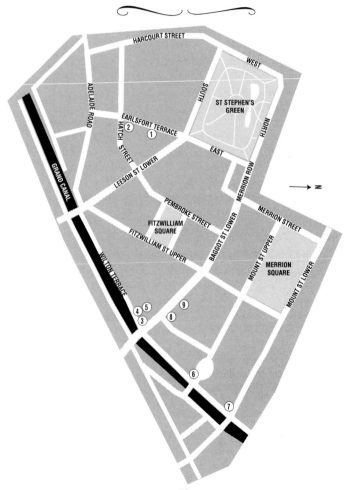

Hotel Conrad International (1) boasts several decorative sculptures and other features.

PEACE COMES DROPPING SLOW is the title for the lovely tiered fountain with flocks of circling birds. The words are from the poem by W.B. Yeats, 'The Lake Isle of Innisfree'. By Colm Brennan and Noel Kidney.

Close behind the fountain is the bronze spiral, THE AWAKENING, by Linda Brunker.

In the passageway between here and Leeson Street are the massive bronze BIO-DYNAMICS by Michael Warren and the mural THE RIVERS OF TIME by Alexandra Wejchert.

All 1989/1990.

2. THE KISS

Farther south, at the corner of Earlsfort Terrace and Lower Hatch Street. Not a passionate embrace this, but a tender and reserved exchange. By Rowan Gillespie, 1989.

BY THE CANAL

T here is a small cluster of memorials and public sculptures by the Grand Canal, particularly in the vicinity of Baggot Street Bridge.

Of the three memorial benches by the canal lock, two are dedicated to Patrick Kavanagh and one to Percy French.

3. PATRICK KAVANAGH

Oh! commemorate me where there is water
Canal water preferably
So stilly greeny in the heart of summer.

wrote poet Patrick Kavanagh (1904-67) who lived nearby for many years. His wish has been carried out in the shape of two separate seats on the canal bank. On one, the life-size bronze figure of Kavanagh relaxes in front of the small Mespil Park (1991). On the opposite bank, a stone seat had already been placed ('just a canal-bank seat for the passer-by') by his friends shortly after his death.

4.   PERCY FRENCH

Another stone bench commemorates Percy French (1854-1920), the much-loved songwriter, artist and engineer who abandoned his professional career to dedicate himself to the more important business of keeping people amused. The bench faces across the canal towards Mespil Road where he lived in No. 35. The legend reads:

> *Remember me is all I ask*
> *And yet*
> *If remembrance prove a task*
> *Forget.*

In the courtyard of Wilton Park House, the building behind Wilton Park, is MAN ON TRESTLE (5). It represents man's precarious progress through life. By Carolyn Mulholland, 1987.

Close to where Mount Street Crescent meets the canal and behind Saint Stephen's Church ('The Pepper Canister'), there is an endearing ghost of old Dublin – a child swings on a lamp-post, bringing memories of days when computer games were unheard of. The sculptor, Derek A. Fitzsimons (1988), calls it MEMORIES OF MOUNT STREET (6).

Further along the canal, at the corner of Lower Mount Street, is a STEEL TOWER (7), echoing a mediaeval Round Tower. By Edward Delaney, 1976.

Inland (westwards) from the canal, on Lower Baggot Street, close to its junction with Herbert Street, a black-robed figure of a nun extends a protective arm to a figure with baby (8). This is the original House of Mercy built by Catherine McAuley (1778-1841), who founded the Order of the Sisters of Mercy in 1831. The building is now the Mercy International Centre.

Farther along Lower Baggot Street, the Bank of Ireland boasts two fine modern sculptures (9). In front of the building, REFLECTIONS by Michael Bulfin, in painted steel, represents shafts of sunlight. An untitled STEEL STRUCTURE by John Burke is by the building's side. Both 1975.

Dublin Castle Area and Westwards

This area is a little out of the centre of town, but is interesting insofar as it is the oldest part of the city and has a great flavour of history. There are few older monuments, strangely enough, but there is a scattering of modern ones. But first, begin on the opposite side of the river from Temple Bar, across the Halfpenny Bridge, at Liffey Street.

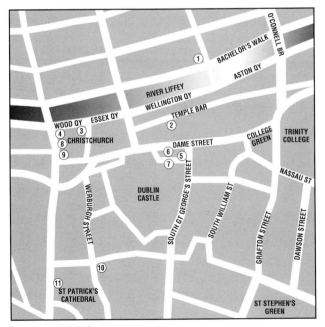

1. MEETING PLACE

The Meeting Place is a welcome stopping-place, already, apparently, occupied by two tired ladies of uncertain age, their shopping bags at their feet. But there is room for you too. The ladies are known unkindly as 'the Hags with the Bags' but in fact are regarded with much affection. By Jakki McKenna, 1988.

... then cross over the Halfpenny Bridge to Temple Bar.

2. TEMPLE BAR

PAVEMENT PATTERNS. Notice the designs on some of the granite kerbstones in this area. They relate to individual premises and their wares. By Rachel Joynt, 1989.

On the island between Asdill's Row and Merchant's Arch, the bronze PALM TREE SEAT by Vincent Browne (1992) is

intended as 'an oasis amidst the hurly burly of city life'. At least it allows rest for weary feet.

The HISTORIC SEAT at the corner of Fownes Street Upper and Cecilia Street, also of bronze, has wood-like carvings of ships, echoing fragments found here during excavations. The bench informs us that Temple Bar dates from 1707 and was named after Sir William Temple (1554-1628). By Betty Maguire, 1992.

3. BÁITE

At Wood Quay, a little further upriver. Dublin grew from a Viking settlement on the Liffey. The fact is commemorated by a resting-spot in the shape of a half-submerged Viking long-boat. 'Báite' means 'drowned' in Irish, though locally the sculpture is referred to as 'the boat which won't float'. By Betty Maguire, 1988.

4. WOOD QUAY

The massive wooden structure outside the Civic Offices, reaching like a tree towards the sky, marks the site of the original Wood Quay of the infant Dublin, begun in the ninth century. Some fragments of that original quay were uncovered in excavations over the past two decades or so. By Michael Warren, 1985.

5. TREE/CHAIR

At the corner of South Great George's Street and Dame Street, this whimsical bronze offers a pause and even a little leafy shade for weary monument-spotters. By Carolyn Mulholland, 1988.

6. On Dame Street, close to the City Hall, a small decorative corner is rather grandiously called the MILLENNIUM GARDEN. The three somewhat weather-beaten classical figures standing around the pool represent the crafts of wood, metal and stone. They originally graced the skyline of the building at Earlsfort Terrace which housed the Dublin Exhibition of Arts, Industries and Manufactures of 1872 and which is now the National Concert Hall.

7. INCOMMUNICADO

Tucked away in Cork Hill, by the western side of the City Hall, is the Conference Hall of Dublin Castle. In its moat stands this two-piece black granite sculpture. The ambivalent

movement of the two pieces, toward and away from each other, is a fair comment on modern communications. By Eileen McDonagh, 1989.

8. VIKING SITE

Early Viking settlements were in the vicinity of Christchurch Cathedral. On its north side, beside Winetavern Street (the street descending to the river), a full-size plan of a typical early Viking building site is marked out on the pavement. An explanatory plaque is on the wall nearby.

On other pavements in the area, including the one leading around the back of Christchurch, a series of bronze slabs shows replicas of artefacts which were excavated in the area. By Rachel Joynt, 1992.

Dublin's Viking age is brought to life in the nearby 'Dublinia' Centre.

9. THE PEACE PARK

Across the street, at the corner of Nicholas Street and Christchurch Place, the small oasis with its ornamental pool symbolises Dublin as a place dedicated to the pursuit of international peace. It incorporates a sculptured TREE OF LIFE and quotations from the work of W.B. Yeats and Patrick Kavanagh. By Colm Brennan and Leo Higgins, 1988.

(At time of going to press, the Peace Park has suffered from vandalism so its present condition can't be vouched for.)

10. JOHN FIELD

On the corner of Bride Street and Golden Lane, facing the railings of St Patrick's Park, is a small monument to the composer John Field (1782-1837) who was born nearby. Field, who is credited with the invention of the nocturne, performed throughout Europe and died in Moscow in 1837. By Colm Brennan and Leo Higgins, 1988.

11. ST PATRICK'S PARK

In the park which surrounds St Patrick's Cathedral is THE LIBERTY BELL, evocative of the bells associated with early Christian monasteries. There is a strong tradition that St Patrick himself was baptised at a well in the park. The spot is now marked by a stone near the Patrick Street Gate. By Vivienne Roche, 1988.

In niches along the back wall of the park is a LITERARY PARADE, a series of plaques commemorating some of Ireland's major writers, including Jonathan Swift (1667-1745) who was Dean of St Patrick's from 1713 until his death. By Colm Brennan and John Coll, 1988.

The group of bronze cones on the pavement outside the railings is called SENTINEL by the artist, Vivienne Roche. They echo and resonate with the space and architecture – a commendable alternative to the usual bollards used by Dublin Corporation to discourage parking.

THE GARDEN OF REMEMBRANCE

lthough a little distance out of the city centre, it would be a pity not to draw attention to this most elaborate of memorials, a 20-acre site on the banks of the Liffey at Islandbridge (buses 25, 25A or 26 from Middle Abbey Street).

The Garden of Remembrance was designed by Sir Edwin Lutyens and commemorates the almost 50,000 Irishmen who died in World War I. A great central cross is flanked by pavilions; there are pools, terraces, fountains and pergolas, all of noble proportions. The massive construction work was undertaken completely by hand in order to give as much employment as possible at the time (the 1930s) and the workforce was made up of ex-soldiers, half and half from the British and Irish armies.

The Gardens fell into decay for a period and were greatly vandalised. The Office of Public Works eventually took the place in hand, thoroughly refurbishing and replanting it. It is now a most impressive site, a place of calm, dignity and beauty. Very much worth a visit.

Across the river, the great 62-metre (205-feet) WELLINGTON TESTIMONIAL rises above the Phoenix Park; it is the tallest obelisk in Europe and, in fact, one of the tallest anywhere. Designed by Sir Robert Smirke, it was begun in 1817 and completed only in 1861. The reliefs on the faces of the plinth are cast from the bronze of captured Napoleonic cannon. As if not big enough already, the memorial was to include an equestrian statue of the Iron Duke beside the obelisk, but that plan was abandoned, possibly because funds ran out.

There are various arguments as to the birth-place of Arthur Wellesley, first Duke of Wellington (1769-1852), but the strongest claim appears to be for 24 Upper Merrion Street in Dublin. The story goes that somebody once referred to him as an Irishman, to which he retorted: 'If you are born in a stable, does that make you a horse?'

Legend has it that a celebratory banquet was held in a vault underneath the obelisk on its completion, and that when the thoroughly inebriated committee left, they sealed the vault behind them, forgetting that the servants were still inside. There is no record of its being opened to find out.